UNSHAKABLE

The DBT Workbook
for Resilient Teens

Stronger Every Day: An Engaging 6-Month Path to Emotional Balance,
Self-Confidence, & Anxiety Relief

Cross Border Books

TABLE OF CONTENTS

Introduction

Every time I read the new statistics on teen mental health I can't help but cringe. Young adults have been expressing that they don't feel great about the world they live in or who they are. Headlines like, "Teens are more stressed than adults," and "Young adults experience a significant rise in major depression," have me wondering, What is it that has our amazing teens feeling so down?

As one of these young adults, I'm sure that you're sitting there waiting for the one thing every adult blames—social media. Now, before you roll your eyes, I'd like you to know that I'm also not 100% on board with the idea that all of the things going wrong have to do with comparing yourself to others online. I do, however, think that social media plays some role in the issues young adults like you are facing, and I'm not alone because teens agree.

In a survey of teens aged 14 to 19, around half said that being online made them feel bad about themselves (Divecha, 2017). But it's not as simple as that—because life never is—and other teens say that spending less time in person and not having to deal with other people face-to-face meant they had fewer pressures and stresses to deal with (Twenge et al., 2018). Confusing, isn't it?

What we can gather from all the studies on social media is that there is some evidence that being online a lot may harm you. But, generally speaking, the research zig zags while scientists test and argue with each other, and the number of teens who aren't coping continues to rise. What the adults all agree on is that heavy online use—

including gaming—is damaging. Having said that, no one can say whether or not it's the real problem teens are dealing with.

As a parent, I think I've become pretty decent at keeping screen time to healthy limits. Of course, this leads me back to the main question: "What is causing young adults so much emotional and psychological pain?"

I did a lot of research when writing this book and I think I've uncovered the issue, at least in part, and it begins with how much of the world's problems you're taking on yourself. As you enter your teen years, changes start to happen in your brain that draw your attention outward. This process means you're looking beyond your family and becoming aware of the bigger issues in the world. You see, young adults become more aware of the world around the age of 14. It's not that you don't know the world existed before then, it's just the trouble and stresses of the society you're living in don't bother you much because the adults will take care of it.

The world is stressful! But it's not more stressful than when your parents or grandparents grew up. There was war, poverty, and much stricter rules back then, and kids were meant to be seen and not heard. So what gives?

Let's go back a moment to the social media studies. There's a whole lot of emphasis being placed on how teens compare themselves to each other online but it seems as if no one is looking at *exposure*. Modern teens are not as protected from the world outside anymore. In the past, the news came via newspaper, radio broadcast, or television. Kids only knew what their parents and teachers told them. When bad things were happening, parents took the time to update themselves on world events when their kids were safely tucked in bed, at school, or chilling outdoors. In other words, the generations before you weren't constantly being exposed to all of the negative things in the world.

As a teen nowadays, you have all of the scary, bad things happening shoved in your faces, and while you might not feel like all of these things are affecting you, they are. You see, your brain is a wonderful organ and it absorbs information all the time—even if you're not aware of it. In other words, you're being exposed to issues surrounding societal problems, climate change, financial troubles, and sexual harassment at least once a day. Plus, you're exposed to these problems alongside the usual teen stuff—like trying to become independent, social belonging, the fear of missing out (FOMO), peer pressure, unrealistic schedules, a changing body and mind, and so on—that's a lot to have to deal with.

You're in the middle of a perfect storm that causes stress and anxiety. Very few adults understand that it's really difficult to cope when your brain simply isn't developed enough to handle all of this stuff.

Heck! Most adults aren't equipped to deal with the state of the world and the stress it causes them. It's pretty tough to try and remain positive and upbeat when it feels like everything is too much, and this problem is where dialectical behavior therapy (DBT) can help. For better or worse, this way of life and the stressors you feel are here to stay, so you need to find ways to cope with the stuff that is happening. Some of these things are a rite of passage. Every teenager before you was exposed to it in some way or form, but modern teens just have it tougher, which means you need a unique set of skills that those previous teens didn't need.

You may feel like you don't need therapy right now, but DBT is so much more than lying on a shrink's sofa and talking about your problems. It gives you skills that can help you manage your feelings of stress as well as the information you need to improve relationships, build emotional intelligence skills, and build a healthy identity.

When reading *Unshakable: The DBT Workbook for Resilient Teens*, you're going to learn all of these skills by completing fun (and relevant) exercises. We'll give you the tools you need to deal with

- peer pressure and making decisions for yourself.

- finding out who you want to become.

- feeling like you're not good enough.

- dealing with FOMO and learning how to turn it into the joy of missing out (JOMO).

O saying no to the things that are not good for you (drugs, alcohol, and other risky behaviors).

O understanding and communicating your big feelings.

O becoming a pro at the skills you need to be fully independent.

When creating this book I was very careful not to be, "yet another adult" who put together a bunch of worksheets because I thought you *needed* them. Instead, I've consulted with teens of all ages to find out what it is that *you* need to navigate the world and live a balanced life. I wanted to create a book that would not only help you make sense of your young adult years but also provide you with the tools you need to

O calm your body and mind so that you can think rationally.

O improve the way you communicate your needs.

O solve problems with critical thinking and proactivity.

O boost your self-esteem with great habits.

We've done the hard work so that we can answer your questions—even the hard ones—and it is my sincere hope that once you've reached the end of this book you have all of the tools you need to navigate life.

CHAPTER 1

What is Dialectical Behavioral Therapy?

I've never been one to mince words or waste time, and because of that, we're going to dive into the nitty gritty of DBT immediately.

DBT might sound like a complicated, boring adult concept but trust me when I say, it's not! I like to think of DBT as the ultimate life hack toolkit that is specifically designed to help you learn the skills you need to navigate this rollercoaster ride that is modern teendom. Like everything else in life, how boring—or interesting—something is comes down to how it's presented. I've always taken on life with a bit of a sense of humor and a whole lot of curiosity for this adventure we're all on, so I'm going to encourage you to do the same as you read through this chapter. This chapter is going to be the only one with the "sciency-type stuff" in it—it's important to know what DBT is.

So what is DBT, and why should you care about it?

I like to think of DBT as a secret weapon—the curl on the forehead and billowing cape that transforms average Clark Kent into planet-saving Superman. It allows you to take on all the tricky stuff life throws your way, helps you navigate your big emotions, and gives you the confidence to develop into an assertive, capable young adult.

You can think about it this way: DBT exercises are the undetectable hack you use in a game called "Real Life," and DBT gives you some of the coolest power-ups to complete levels and play the game like a boss!

In the late 1970s, Dr. Marsha Linehan cracked the code on how to equip people with the skills they needed to manage their emotions and relationships with ease. She was basically the Einstein of feelings and personal relationships, and she combined other older forms of therapy with some pretty awesome life hacks—just like the Real Life game.

If we break down DBT, it becomes easier to understand why it's such an amazing tool for young adults to learn. Let's take a look.

D stands for "dialectical," a big, fancy word that basically means the balance of opposite things. Think of the word dialectical like when you need to choose between pizza and sushi for supper—these foods are polar opposites but really amazing so it becomes a tough choice, right?

B is for "behavior." The skills you learn with DBT help you to change your actions so that you can become a kinder human being to yourself and to others.

T is for "therapy." Don't freak out! You're not going to be lying on a couch and spilling your problems or feelings (although there's nothing wrong with that if you need or want it.) When we speak about DBT, we're referring directly to your journey in life, and therapy is your personal guide to understanding yourself and the world around you.

Just like every other superhero, DBT comes with some hidden superpowers that you're going to learn and use so that you can become the Superman of your own life. These powers include the following examples:

- **Mindfulness:** Mindfulness is the shield that protects you from stress and helps you to stay focused on what is happening in the present moment. Imagine living in a world where faceplanting while texting is no longer a life-changing embarrassing moment—this is the power of mindfulness.

○ **Emotional regulation:** This phrase refers to the ability to be patient and appreciate taking a beat when you feel like it's all too much and your feelings are going to get the better of you. Think of emotional regulation as the superstrength that keeps the rollercoaster of life on its tracks.

○ **Interpersonal effectiveness:** These are big words, I know! Think of this phrase as the ability to have conversations that don't turn into epic fails. It's the ability to move with stealth through life, handling any social situation with confidence.

○ **Stress tolerance**: Look, real life can be a pain in the "you-know-what" a lot of the time, but stress tolerance helps you to fortify yourself against these challenges without losing your cool. It's a sword that helps you to cut through the tangled branches that are on your path from time to time.

Now that you know what DBT is, we can move on to what it can do for you and how it will help you discover your own superpowers.

What DBT Can Do for You

One of the questions I hear most often from teens is, "What can DBT do for me?" This question is a reasonable thing to ask, and my standard answer is: "It can do a whole lot!" This answer is pretty vague, so let's get into the specifics.

1. You learn to master your emotions: How you feel can sometimes be an overwhelming rollercoaster ride that can feel like there are no brakes, no operator, and nothing to steer you in the direction of safety. DBT teaches you how to manage your emotions in a healthy way.

2. DBT shows you how to say goodbye to stress: That's right, DBT teaches you to manage stress like a *boss*, dodging curveballs and unlocking a winning gameplay when it comes to things like exams, relationship drama, and that one friend who makes you feel like trash even when they say, "No offense."

3. Communication mastery: You'll be shown how to improve your relationships with proper communication, confidence, and conflict resolution. Remember

that time you got into it with your BFF over the last slice of pizza? Well, say "sayonara" to those situations because DBT helps you communicate like a pro!

4. DBT gives you the tools you need to boost your self-esteem: DBT helps you navigate those awkward moments in life with ease. With a great sense of self-worth and esteem, you can begin to walk through life with your head held high, take on challenges with a different mindset, and embrace your uniqueness.

5. It turns you into a stress destroyer: Bobby Iceman will have nothing on you once you begin to complete your DBT exercises! Life may be a pressure cooker of stress at times but you'll be shown healthy ways to blow off steam, handle tough situations, and become the Zen Master of calmness, even when things get tough.

6. DBT silences nasty thoughts: With DBT, you can learn how to quiet your inner critic, showing them the timeout corner in the recesses of your mind. No more listening to self-limiting beliefs and intrusive thoughts—you'll know how to challenge and silence this stressful part of being a human.

7. Finally, DBT hands you the key to the coolest gifts life has to offer—balance and inner joy: You no longer need to tiptoe and tightrope walk through life because you'll have the skills to learn acceptance and know when to change.

Okay, teen, we're almost at the fun part. Let's look at the final bit of information you need to know before diving into your DBT exercises.

Why Are DBT Exercises and Worksheets Better Than Talk Therapy?

Another bit of info I would like to share with you is why completing DBT exercises might be more beneficial than traditional talk therapy.

The first thing I'd like you to know is that talk therapy is super useful. If you're already in some form of therapy, that's great! You can use this workbook as an added extra to help you level up and navigate life with a little more understanding alongside your current therapy sessions.

If you're not in therapy and feel like you need it, speak to a grown-up in your life and ask them to arrange an appointment for you. Or, you can head to your local community center—they usually have more information on free services. This workbook is not intended to replace therapy. It's designed to give you a fun, safe way to learn awesome skills that will improve your life.

But not everyone feels like they need to have formal therapy sessions and I totally support that if you're being honest with yourself. Regardless of your reasons for reading this book, you may be asking, "Why exercises and worksheets?" We're going to answer this question for you next.

The first thing you need to know is that people learn better through action than information. This concept sounds a bit complicated, but let me explain. When you're actually doing something and not just talking about it, your brain becomes more engaged. Talking about your problems and the solutions to them is great, but unless you actually get up and do something about it, the problem is never going to go away. Imagine you spent your whole life talking about riding a bike but never actually got on it to ride it. You wouldn't expect that you were going to stay upright, would you?

DBT lets you build the mental muscles of your mind while equipping you with the practical skills you need to deal with the real world. And here's the thing about these exercises... You can take them out into the world immediately, practicing them as you go along. Speaking about the things that are troubling you provides you with a roadmap to a solution, and DBT exercises give you the keys so that you can drive to that solution!

But DBT isn't a whole bunch of "what ifs." They're real-world skills that can be applied to real-world situations so that you can navigate the challenges you will inevitably face. Imagine getting an exclusive sneak peek to the next level of your life—it's going to be a lot easier leveling up if you already know how to handle what's coming, right? This provides you with a whole lot of independence as well as the confidence to speak about the things you're unsure of. You can take charge of your own mental health but still know where your limits are and when to ask for help.

The final question you may have is what you have to do and why is this book for you. Let's begin with what you have to do.

So the obvious answer to this question is, "Complete the exercises"—but it's not that simple. You need to pay attention to the information you're being given and apply it consistently. I mean, you wouldn't learn to drive a car and only half listen or half practice. The same goes for DBT. You need to pay attention, immerse yourself in the exercises, and be honest about what you're learning and then you need to go ahead and do what you have learned.

The next thing you need to do is track your progress. This part is one of the best things about DBT workbooks because you have a black-and-white (or however colorful you want it to be) record of your successes and what might need to improve.

That's it! Now you know what DBT is, what it can do for you, and how it differs from talking about your problems. When you are ready, turn the page so that you can unlock your secret weapon for leveling up in life with customized exercises and therapeutic awesomeness that solve the issues that are relevant to you, teen.

CHAPTER 2

Is It Me? Am I the Drama? Emotional Regulation in Your Teen Years

Aaah... Emotions... those weird feelings that start in your brain and cause feelings in your body. They can feel like they're making you behave in a certain way and feel terrible after you slammed your door in your sibling's face because they breathed in your direction.

Sometimes you wish you didn't have emotions at all, or, at the very least, you only want to experience the good ones. Here's the thing about emotions—they're super important parts of your everyday life. But (and this is a big but) they can also change from moment to moment when you're a teen.

A lot of things can affect your emotions when you're in your teen years. Hormones, not enough support, stress, your thoughts, and the changing structure of your brain can all have your emotions hit the turbo button on a neverending rollercoaster of ups and downs.

Your emotions are a leftover from evolution when big bads were lurking around every corner and the survival of the human race depended on you finding someone to reproduce with. Now, modern people don't have many of these physical threats, like sabertoothed tigers or mammoths, and we don't have to look far to find a couple of people we would like to date. Sure, there are other bad things happening, but for the most part, your life isn't in immediate danger as often as your caveperson ancestors.

However, your brain doesn't know that danger isn't imminent and that people have evolved, so it produces the same strong emotional responses it did all those hundreds of years ago. There's good news, though: You don't need to be a slave to your emotions.

The goal of regulating your emotions is firstly to make sure you're not strapped into the most unpredictable rollercoaster ride of your life. Secondly, when you can manage your emotions, you are less likely to turn to stuff like drugs and alcohol to try and drown out the feelings you're having.

Identifying Your Emotions

Let's get into identifying your emotions. What you know after reading the opening of this chapter is that emotions are the reactions or responses we have that are brought on by memories, actions, thoughts, or circumstances. When you feel an emotion, it happens in your brain. However, emotions can also cause physical reactions and sensations. These sensations and reactions can be the sweaty hands, blushing, heart racing, and shaking that happen when you're scared or anxious. Or, they can be the laughter and tears experienced when you're really happy.

Science and psychology are undecided on how many human emotions there are. Some say that there are only six primary emotions and everything else that you feel is a mixture of more than one emotion. For example, disgust and anger create shame or disrespect. How many emotions there are doesn't really matter though, especially if you know how to name your emotions so that you can begin to manage them. Let's take a look at these common emotions so that you can begin to label them.

Using the table below, have a look at the emotion and the possible accompanying physical sensations. In the blank columns, tick whether or not you can label this emotion and the physical sensations you feel.

Emotion	Physical sensation	I have experienced this	I feel... when I experience this
Joy	Faster heartbeat and breathing, body feels warmer, feeling tingles in fingers and toes		
Sadness	Tight chest or throat, burning or watering eyes, skin might feel sensitive, may feel anxious or jittery		
Anger	Face and body get hot, shaking, heavy or slow deep breaths, not feeling present, fast heartbeat		
Grief	Tightness in the chest and feeling of heaviness in the body, tearfulness, pain in the stomach and joints, headache or pressure in the head		
Happiness	Racing heart or slower heartbeat, pleasant tenseness in the face, or complete relaxation, butterflies in the stomach, may feel like crying		

Shame/ guilt	Hollow feeling in the stomach, racing thoughts, shaky hands, or weakness in legs and arms, may feel fear, anger, sadness
Fear	Racing thoughts, increased heart rate, warm feeling in the face and body, hollow feeling in the stomach, shaking, feeling like you want to run away, may feel anger
Anxiety/ stress	Increased heartbeat and breathing, gasping for breath, butterflies or pain in the stomach, headache, tense muscles, feeling angry, feeling sad or tearful, body aches, may even feel feverish and sick

If you're going through the list above and you're confused, don't worry, emotions are *seriously* confusing—even for adults! That's why you can try to understand them but a lot of the time won't because they're about as irrational as the sabertooth your brain thinks still exists.

What is important to remember when it comes to emotions is this fact: They can't be controlled, but they can be managed and turned into your own, personal superpower.

I Named Them, So How Do I Manage Them?

Once you know what emotions you're feeling it becomes way easier to begin regulating and managing them. But what are emotional regulation skills?

Your emotions come from your thoughts, feelings, and reactions to the things that are happening around you. The things that cause your emotions are called stimuli. For example, let's say you walk into a store you're familiar with and there are a couple of people but everyone is calm and no one looks up or notices you. The people, the store, and the familiarity are all stimuli. Your brain will take these external cues in and it will trigger a thought or memory that says, "I like this place, my memories here are good." Or, "I know this place, last time I was here people judged me." The thoughts and memories that your brain associates with stimuli are endless—some of them might be true, some might be only slightly true, and some might be made up.

Now, this part is where it gets a little more confusing. Stimuli can be external or internal or a combination of both. This breakdown means you can have an emotion purely by thinking about something or recalling a memory. What's worse, you can experience an emotion for something imaginary, not true, and 100% made up! Eek! Right?

Your brain simply doesn't know what is true and what is not when it comes to internal and external stimuli and it relies on this area in your brain called the prefrontal cortex (PFC) to say, "Yeah this could be true. No this is not true, or yes, this is true." There's a challenge for you as a teen: Your prefrontal cortex is not developed yet. Because your PFC is one of the last areas of your brain to mature and develop, you're dealing with a whole lot of adult thoughts but your brain just isn't equipped to deal with this stuff. This doesn't mean you're doomed to ride the rollercoaster of your emotions until your brain catches up, though.

Your brain has this amazing ability called "plasticity." What this concept means is that your brain can learn, physically grow (or shrink), and develop at all stages of your life. Just like when you were a toddler learning to tie your shoes until you didn't need to even think about how to get them tied anymore, you can practice regulating your emotions until it's second nature. But, this doesn't happen by pushing down what you feel or ignoring the reasons you're feeling the way you are.

How Your DBT Exercises Will Work

You'll notice that the exercises from this point on are labeled with week numbers. The reason for this labeling is that it allows you to set aside time to complete each exercise and get the hang of it.

Each chapter will have three exercises and a bonus activity like the one above on labeling emotions. All you need to do is go through the instructions for these exercises and then tick them off once you've completed each DBT session.

So what are the rules?

Well, that's the coolest thing about DBT—there aren't any! But, there are two really important things you need to remember:

1. Be honest with yourself at all times. There's no sense in lying to yourself about the stuff in these exercises because lies are only going to stop you from progressing.

2. If at any point you feel like it's too much, like you're going to hurt yourself (or others), or that you just can't carry on, speak to a trusted grown-up who can help you.

And that's it! So have fun and let's dive in.

DBT Exercises Weeks 1 to 4

The exercises below have been selected specifically for you, teen. Each exercise is not only fun but will help you to become a master of your emotions.

Here's how.

Exercise 1 teaches you to build tolerance so that you're not blowing your top at the first sign of stress, rejection, or resistance.

Exercise 2 provides you with one of the most powerful tools ever to be discovered—mindfulness. Using mindfulness you can step out of the past and future and live in the right now!

Exercise 3 provides you with a visual reference of how emotions can change every day. When you can see how changeable your feelings are, you can uncover patterns that you could be contributing to.

Exercise 1—Taking a Beat

Because the emotional centers of your brain work great in your teen years (I know it can be a pain), but your PFC needs time to catch up, you're going to need to train yourself to learn how to pause when you're feeling an emotion.

This process works for two reasons:

1. Sometimes, your PFC just needs a moment to rationalize the stimuli you're experiencing.

2. Your emotions are temporary.

I know it can feel like your emotions linger all day—like that time you forgot your homework and felt down the whole day. The reality is that emotions last no more than three minutes. What happens after you experience an emotion is all conscious.

What this concept means is that your brain is finding a way to maintain how you're feeling because you either haven't challenged the original emotion with a rational thought or you're choosing to stay in your feels.

This prolonged state is called your "mood" and works in this way:

You wake up, get to school, and realize you forgot your homework. You feel angry with yourself and anxious that you'll get into trouble. You react by panicking and trying to copy a friend's work so you have something to hand in. Now, you're feeling even more anxious because your thoughts are racing with things like, *I'm going to get caught out and fail, My friend is going to get suspended for helping me,* or *My parents are going to ground me for life*! These thoughts keep going, and while you're not still experiencing an emotion, your mood is low and anxious all day.

Alternatively, instead of panicking, you could take a beat and allow your PFC to catch up. Instead of reacting, you think about how you could rectify this situation. You're mindful of the fact that this situation is temporary and that you made a mistake. Your thoughts say, *You know what, I messed up, I'll talk to my teacher and see if there is a way to fix this.* You confidently speak to your teacher, present solutions, and accept responsibility for your actions. Your mood is lifted and your emotions pass.

What You'll Need

- ⭕ your journal or a piece of paper

- ⭕ a pen or pencil

- ⭕ an open mind

- ⭕ a timer of sorts

Directions

- ⭕ Clear your exercise space, making sure it's clutter-free.

- ⭕ Gather your exercise materials.

- ⭕ Turn your phone face down and put it on silent—if you're using your phone as a timer, you can complete this step once you have set the timer.

- ⭕ Switch off all other electronic devices.

- ⭕ Set your timer to 10 minutes.

- ⭕ Begin by closing your eyes and recalling a time when you had an immediate emotional reaction.

- ⭕ Write this situation down.

- ⭕ Now ask yourself the following questions:

- What emotion did I feel?

- What were the physical sensations I felt?

- How did I react?

- How could I have handled the situation?

○ Take a moment to reflect on what you have written. Do you feel any emotions right now as you are completing this exercise?

○ Now, I'd like you to stand up.

○ Begin to pace your room or wherever you're doing your exercise.

○ Without thought, freeze—you can even tell yourself to freeze real loud.

○ Don't move a muscle—just stand there frozen.

○ Take a deep breath and observe the things that are stimulating you.

- What are your thoughts right now?

- How do you feel?

- Are you experiencing an emotion?

○ Take another deep breath, return to your journal or page, and write the answers to the above questions down.

○ Rationalize the answers to your questions by answering these questions:

- Are my thoughts 100% true?

- If they are true, what can I do about them?

- Does my mood reflect the situation or my thoughts?

- If I experienced an emotion, what was it?

○ Take another deep breath, close your journal, or file your paper away.

○ If your timer hasn't gone off yet, you can sit quietly and contemplate your exercise or get up and move about to release your energy.

Exercise 2—Yoda'esque Mindfulness

There's a lot of talk about mindfulness (and for good reason), but it's a bit of a complicated process to fully understand. Mindfulness is the ability to pay full attention to what is happening right now, in the present moment.

That means taking the time (beat) to notice what is going on, what you're doing, and what your thoughts are. Sometimes, mindfulness happens naturally, like when you're picking out what to wear, playing an instrument, or concentrating on a task. Mindfulness, most of the time, leads to what is called a flow state.

Now, this flow state is amazing because it happens when all the areas of your brain are working together perfectly alongside your body. In other words, your thoughts, emotions, and feelings line up with your actions and things happen without too much effort.

So why do teens need mindfulness?

Well, being mindful helps you to pay more attention to the stuff that is affecting you, allows you to be less distracted, lets your brain absorb more information, helps you stay calm under stress, and ensures you get your tasks done quickly and properly.

But that's not all. When it comes to your emotions and mood, mindfulness helps you to

○ manage your emotions better so you don't blow your top or dissolve into tears.

○ learn the skills you need to be self-controlled.

○ regulate your emotions.

○ increase how much you enjoy the stuff you're doing.

In social situations and relationships, mindfulness is great for helping you to listen to others when they're speaking, to be more patient with others and yourself, and to improve your relationships because you understand others and yourself better.

Mindfulness is an amazing superpower that most people only learn much later in life and often when they are in a crisis or just plain unhappy with their lives. Learning how to be mindful in your teen years means you don't have to go through all the hard stuff *before* the superpower, and that's pretty amazing, I think!

What You'll Need

- a timer
- a clear, distraction-free space
- your journal or a piece of paper
- a pen or pencil

Directions

- Clear your space and make sure it is distraction-free.
- Set your timer for three minutes—you should add two minutes per week until you reach 10 minutes.
- Sit comfortably on the floor or on a chair.
- Keep your spine straight.
- Place your hands on your thighs, palm down.
- Inhale deeply and close your eyes.
- As you exhale, bring your attention to your breath.
- Inhale and notice how your chest rises—try not to pay attention to anything other than your breath.

○ If you find your thoughts wandering, that's fine and perfectly normal.

○ Observe these thoughts and try not to judge them. Simply hear what they're saying and let them float away, bringing your attention back to your breathing.

○ When your timer goes off, try to remember some of your thoughts—if you can't, don't worry!

○ Write down any thoughts you remember in your journal.

○ Once a week, read over your thoughts to see if a pattern is forming so that you can challenge the negative ones.

Exercise 3—Splash and Dash

You can experience different emotions during the day, and all of these different emotions can affect your mood if you let them. An amazing way to keep track of your emotions so that you can see what situations are triggering certain emotions is with the Splash and Dash exercise.

So how does this exercise work exactly?

The human brain will usually tie an emotion or feeling to a color. Not everyone is the same, though. I might see red and think *power* or *bravery*, and you might see red and think *anger* or *danger*. For some people, green may make them feel calm, and for others, it may even create feelings of aggression.

What you need to do is use your Yoda'esque mindfulness to figure out what a color feels like to you. Once you know this little bit of information, you can use it to uncover a whole lot about not only how your emotions have changed during the day but also if certain things are triggering you to feel not so great about yourself. This process gives you insight, which is a big word for being able to spy on emotions.

When you know what is triggering your emotions, and you can label your emotions, it becomes much easier for you to manage them.

What You'll Need

○ a large piece of paper, cardboard, or canvas

○ a paintbrush

○ paint in different colors

○ a jar of water

○ a rag or scrap cloth

○ plastic sheeting, an old sheet, or something that will protect your workspace

○ a timer

Directions

○ Clear your space and lay your painting materials out in front of you.

○ Make sure the surfaces surrounding your immediate workspace are covered.

○ Set your timer for 10 minutes

○ Begin your exercise by thinking about how you felt during the day.

○ As soon as you recall an emotion, look over at the colors laid out in front of you.

○ Pick a color that you feel best goes with the emotion you felt.

○ Dip your paintbrush into the color and splash the paint across your page.

○ Dip your brush in water and clean it off.

○ Don't think too much about what is happening on your page—let your thoughts and emotions flow, choosing one color after the next.

○ When your timer goes off, clean your brush off, put away your paints, and allow your paper/cardboard/canvas to dry.

○ Try not to look at your painting in too much detail until you have completed the full three weeks of your exercise—just keep layering one color on top of the next.

○ At the end of every week, allow your painting to dry and then hang it up.

○ Have a look at how your emotions have changed. Do you see any patterns or do your emotions change a lot? Can you see that your emotions might be messy sometimes but they still come together to create an amazing picture?

Week 1 to 4 Timetable

Monday	Tuesday	Wednesday	Thursday	Friday	Saturday	Sunday
Mindfulness	Mindfulness	Mindfulness	Mindfulness	Mindfulness	Mindfulness	Mindfulness
						Check your journal for thought patterns
Taking a Beat		Taking a Beat		Taking a Beat		
Splash and Dash	Splash and Dash	Splash and Dash	Splash and Dash	Splash and Dash	Splash and Dash	Review Splash and Dash`

You now have all the tools you need to practice managing your emotions. By using the timetable, you can easily start to manage your emotions by practicing your exercises. The best thing about these exercises is that you only need 15 minutes a day to start seeing results.

If you enjoy any of these three exercises and want to continue with them (mindfulness is a particularly great one to continue with), feel free to add them to your daily habits and routine.

CHAPTER 3

No Identity Crisis Here!

If you're not too sure what identity is, don't worry! You're about to understand what exactly the two main types of identity are and why they're important. The exercises in Chapter 3 are going to focus on your self-identity but it's super important that you understand social identity as well because it can affect how you think about yourself.

Okay, so self-identity is who you think you are. It's not a label that you have like brother, sister, or child, but rather who you believe you are. Here's an example of your identity: "I'm creative, funny, and smart!" Your identity grows and changes throughout your whole life and depends on a couple of things including how you want to see yourself and how you want others to see you. That's not to say your whole identity is something you choose. In fact, some of your self-identity comes from social identity.

Your social identity is what others think of you. This identity often comes with a label, and it's not a label you put on yourself but you can choose to adopt it. An example of a social identity would be if you have dark skin and you're labeled Black. Depending on your family and cultural upbringing you might identify as Black or you might not. Your social label may or may not affect your self-identity.

But why does self-identity matter?

If you have a positive self-identity you're going to have high self-esteem, which means you're more likely to feel great about yourself. You'll have a good idea of what your strengths and weaknesses are and can act on your weaknesses so that you can get better in life. With a great self-identity, you learn to love yourself and you make great choices for yourself because no one wants to hurt someone they love. Your mental health also improves when your self-identity is strong and you are more confident in asking for help when you need it.

When you have a positive self-identity and high self-esteem, your relationships improve, your communication skills get better, and you can learn to separate reality from all that stuff you see online. And, you begin to feel happier and more content in your life. Awesome, right?

The Different Parts of Your Self-Identity

Remember when I said that adults are still arguing about the causes of teen anxiety and stress? Well, a lot of this argument revolves around self-identity—and for good reason.

Your self-identity is really important, but as a teen, it is also affected by external factors, including social media. Some schools of thought believe that as many as 66 different factors determine your self-identity. Now, this belief may be true, but there are four key areas of your life that are really, really important. One of these areas is fixed, meaning you have no control over it, and three of them are totally within your control.

Your personality is kinda not within your control, and it is called a fixed trait. The thing about your personality is it's changeable to a certain extent. I know it all sounds confusing, but here's a great example: Let's say you have a jar of white Play-Doh. You play with it and a couple of pieces break off or go missing. The Play-Doh is now smaller, but it is still Play-Doh, right? One day you discover purple Play-Doh at the store and you really like the color, so you buy it, bring it home, and mix it with your white Play-Doh. You now have a larger ball of white and purple Play-Doh. It has swirls of both colors and some of it has mixed to form a new color. Do you still have Play-Doh? Sure you do! It's slightly different but there are still elements of the white. No matter how many layers and sparkles you add to this collection, it's still going to be white Play-Doh on some level.

That's how your personality works. You're born with the foundation of it, but the things you do and experience will add layers to your personality just like the Play-Doh.

The different colors, sparkles, and add-ons are your achievements, values, and beliefs. Some of these elements are easier to get rid of and others mix together with your personality. Your achievements and values are like the purple Play-Doh. You could probably get rid of some of the color if you tried really hard, but there will always be little bits of it left. Your beliefs are the sparkles you add to your Play-Doh. If you don't like them, you simply pick them out and add something new until you do like the look of your Play-Doh. Now, some beliefs may be harder to get rid of than others, but with time and effort, you can get rid of them entirely.

So what have you learned from this example?

Some of the stuff that makes you who you are is fixed but other stuff you can add or take away to improve yourself. It's pretty neat if you ask me!

The exercises in this section are designed to help you add stuff that will help you create a strong sense of identity. They'll also help you take the stuff away that may be not so great for your self-esteem, like limiting beliefs.

Remember when you're doing these exercises that it's really important to be honest about what *you* want for yourself and not what other people or social media pressure you to believe you *need*.

Those Sneaky Limiting Beliefs

Sometimes it can be difficult to uncover the thoughts you have that limit your abilities or drive you to make sketchy decisions. When your thoughts go into overdrive and they're not great or positive thoughts, it can limit you in making decisions that are great for you. There are a couple of super simple ways that you can identify these thoughts and beliefs.

Take a look at the statements below.

- ○ I'm going to look stupid if I start this now.

- ○ I'm never going to have any friends.

- ○ I should have studied harder.

- ○ It's too hard—I could never do that.

These examples are called definitive statements, which means that, on the surface, they look like they can't be challenged. These statements are also what self-limiting beliefs look like. They tell you that you *should* do things, *could have* done something, or *can't* do things even when there are no facts to back up the thought. These thoughts also often revolve around things you have no control over. If you didn't study enough for an exam and you got a low grade, thinking, *I should have studied harder*, won't change the result because you can't go back in time. You could change this by studying better next time but then other limiting beliefs pop up like, *It's too hard* or *I'm stupid*.

Do you see how limiting beliefs just grow and grow and grow if you don't do anything about them?

You'll learn how to challenge these beliefs in the next exercise. For now, let's look at ways you can pick them out of all of the thoughts you have.

Limiting beliefs come in types A, B, and C.

Type A

Type A limiting beliefs are things we don't ever think about challenging. They're the things that are black and white, but we can sometimes get so caught up in them that they can cause obsessions. For example, you know hurting someone is bad but you may have a thought that says you want to hurt someone. You become so upset by this thought that you allow it to fill your mind over and over again until you become so distressed that you do physical things to help you soothe your emotional pain. This situation is an example of how obsessive compulsive disorder (OCD) happens.

These types of self-limiting beliefs are rare but do happen to teens.

Type B

Type B limiting beliefs are more common for teens like you. They're the thoughts we have that can be taken as true but can also be challenged. They form part of what is called your core beliefs. When type B beliefs are positive, they help improve your confidence and self-esteem. When they are negative, they make you feel terrible about yourself. Sometimes you might not even be aware that you're having these thoughts and you need to look out for them to challenge them. For example, you might say, "I'm a funny person," and your behavior would support this statement. Or, you might say "Nobody likes me," and you may close yourself off so that you're not approachable for other people.

Type C

Type C limiting beliefs are the things other people have said or done that affect your confidence in yourself. Teens from helicopter parents or adults who wouldn't let children try out new things when they were younger can instill the belief that the teen can't do hard things. Or, perhaps you were laughed at for tripping and falling at school one day and now you tell yourself that you're clumsy and everyone thinks you're stupid. These types of beliefs are also very common in teens but can be easily identified because they tie back to emotional reactions. "I can't do hard things," for example, will come with feelings of fear or anxiety. The good news is that these types of limiting beliefs can be easily fixed.

Now that you know what kinds of limiting beliefs exist, look at the list below and try to see if you label them A, B, or C, and tick off if you've had any of these thoughts.

Belief/thought	Type A, B, or C	Had this thought, yes or no
I'm not good enough.		
I'm not pretty/good-looking.		
I'm not smart.		
I don't deserve to have...		
I've got the worst luck.		
I always hurt people.		
I'm responsible for...		
I would be successful if...		
I don't belong.		
I will feel loved if...		
I need to be... for people to...		
Some things only happen to me.		
I can't succeed because I am...		
My family has never...		

Answers

1. Type C

2. Type B or C

3. Type B or C

4. Type A or C

5. Type B

6. Type A or C

7. Type A

8. Type B

9. Type C

10. Type A or C

11. Type C

12. Type B

13. Type A or C

14. Type A

Amazing! Now that you are a pro at identifying the types of limiting thoughts. Let's move on to the next set of exercises.

DBT Exercises Weeks 5 to 9

It's time to get to your specifically designed exercises. These activities are to be completed in weeks 5 to 9 and will help you get rid of those limiting beliefs and thoughts, build your self-confidence, and take control of developing a strong identity.

Exercise 4 teaches you how to challenge the beliefs that are limiting you and influencing your behavior. You'll be given a set of questions that can stop these thoughts in their tracks, and if they don't, they will let you know what steps to take next.

Exercise 5 allows you to build self-confidence so that you can overcome those negative thoughts that are holding you back. It shows you the value of proper planning and bestows you with an amazing superpower most adults only learn way later in their lives.

Exercise 6 is designed to teach you how to love yourself, even when you're going through tough times or when you've made a bad decision.

Exercise 4—Unlocking Your Inner Mythbuster

DBT uses elements of another type of therapy called cognitive-behavioral therapy (CBT). When these two types of therapies are combined, it creates a powerful punch against negative thoughts and that annoying inner critic that tells you stuff that just isn't true.

In this exercise, you're going to dive deeper into how you can pick out those negative thoughts that are limiting you. You'll be given a set of super easy questions that will help you to silence these thoughts quickly.

Now, before you begin with these exercises, I want to let you in on a secret—DBT uses a lot of mindfulness when teaching you the skills you need to feel better in this chaotic world. This means it's a good idea to carry on with your mindful practices, even if they're not technically required for weeks 5 to 9.

The other thing I'd like you to know is that it takes a little bit of time and practice to shift your thought patterns. Remember, your brain is wired to think negatively to try and keep you safe from all things primitive and non-existent in the modern world. Don't worry—you're not going to be stuck in this loop forever! All you need to do is commit to unlocking your inner myth-buster every time these thoughts invade your mind.

What You'll Need

- ○ your journal

- ○ a pen or pencil

- ○ or the electronic worksheet below

Directions

- ○ You'll begin with Worksheet 1 which goes deeper into negative thoughts and how they present themselves. All you need to do is read through these thoughts and reflect on a time when you might have thought this way.

○ Next, you'll have a look at Worksheet 2. This worksheet provides you with some easy questions that redirect your brain and challenge these negative thoughts.

○ Truthfully fill in the answers next to each of these questions.

○ Worksheet 3 lets you fill in intrusive or negative thoughts the minute they happen. Filling this worksheet in lets you uncover thought patterns that you might be having. It also allows you to do your exercises at a specific time without having to remember what limiting thoughts you might have had.

Worksheet 1

Column 1 labels the type of limiting thought as well as lets you know some of the words associated with the thought.

Column 2 asks you to name a time when you had this type of thought.

Column 3 is where you'll fill in the emotion that came with the thought.

Column 4 is for what happened after the thought.

For example, I thought everyone would hate me when I started at a new school. I was scared but it turned out everyone was really nice to me.

Type	Circumstance	Emotion	Outcome
Black and white: These are thoughts that say "always, never, every, all the time..." They usually happen with Type A or B beliefs.			

Regret thoughts:
These are the "I would've, could've" thoughts we have where we're living in the past. They come with Type B beliefs.

Mind-reading:
This type of thought is when you think you know how other people feel or think. It's the "people are going to laugh at me" thoughts we sometimes have. These thoughts come with Type B and C beliefs.

Catastrophizing:
These thoughts make us think the worst is going to happen. For example, "Everyone is going to hate me!" These thoughts come from Type A, B, or C beliefs.

Shoulds: These thoughts are a bit different from Regret Thoughts. They're based on judgments of what you think the outcome must be rather than accepting the outcome. These thoughts can come from Type A, B, or C beliefs.

Worksheet 2

Below are some simple questions you can ask when you experience a negative or limiting thought. These questions are really powerful and work by not only redirecting your brain but by uncovering the thought as a total lie. Now, I hear you asking, "What if the thought is true?"

Well, if the thought is true, you now have the perfect chance to change! The beauty of being a human being is that you always have a chance to do better and be better.

Directions

- ○ Begin by writing down your negative thought.

- ○ Next, answer the questions below.

Question	Answer
Is this a black and white, regret, mind-reading, catastrophizing, or shoulds thought?	
Is there any truth to this thought?	
Could I have confused or misinterpreted the situation?	
Would I say this negative thing to a friend or someone I love?	
What would someone I love say if they heard me speaking about myself like this?	
Am I 100% sure that what I am thinking will happen?	
If this thought has happened before, how many times did it happen?	
What is the worst that could happen if this thought came true?	
If this thought did happen what could I do to cope with it?	
Am I working on facts or on the way I feel?	
Could I be confusing "maybe" or "might" with "definitely"?	
Is this thought a fear or simply a hassle?	
What is the best that can happen with preparation and confidence?	

Worksheet 3

Your final worksheet is designed to make notes as a thought happens. It can be used to see if patterns are forming in your thoughts and so that you have all your thoughts collected in one space for your daily DBT exercises.

Situation or trigger	Thought	Emotion on a scale of 1-10

Exercise 5—Who's the Most Confident of Them All? (Spoiler Alert: It's You!)

This simple exercise helps you to see all the amazing, unique, and positive things that exist because you're here on this planet!

All you need to do is take a look at the table and rate the statement every day. Totally Agree (5) is the best mark and Just No (1) is the worst mark.

Statement	Totally Agree (4)	I Guess So (3)	Meh (2)	Just No (1)
I rocked today!				
I sucked today.				
I worked in my strengths.				
I did hard things.				
I did something today that I am proud of!				
I made mistakes.				

I respected

myself today.

I made some

good choices.

I loved myself

no matter what

today.

Right, now that you have rated each of these statements, take a walk on over to the mirror and repeat the following statements.

1.   I rock every day!

2.   It's okay for some parts of my day to suck.

3.   I work within my strengths.

4.   I do hard things.

5.   I am proud of myself.

6.   It's human to make mistakes.

7.   I respect myself.

8.   I make good choices.

9.   I love myself exactly where I am.

Over the next 4 weeks, take note of how your negative thoughts start to up and leave and how much more you become positive.

Exercise 6—The Ultimate Love Triangle: Me, Myself, and I

One of the hardest (and sometimes weirdest) things you learn as you become a teen is that Hollywood and the real world are really different a lot of the time. What you can learn from movies is that the underdog (that's you, teen) often becomes the hero and that with love, just about anything is possible.

The ultimate love triangle doesn't happen on your digital devices and screens though. It happens within you and as you learn to love yourself during all the stages of your life. I know that sometimes it can feel difficult to love yourself but I want you to know that there is nothing wrong with being totally, 100% head over heels for yourself, even when you make mistakes or bad choices. Wanting to get better or to improve doesn't come from a place of not liking who you are—it comes from loving yourself so fiercely that you *need* better for yourself.

Loving yourself is where great self-esteem begins and it's the foundation for building on your confidence until you become super sure that you can make good choices for your growth. But, sometimes your brain gets so caught up in the negative stuff that it can feel difficult to believe in your abilities to do the right thing or to be confident.

Most people, when they are feeling scared or not confident will put on a show. Like an actor or actress, they wear their "mask" and hope that by playing the part, they'll become more confident. It's the whole "fake it 'til you make it" saying and it actually works!

In this exercise, you're going to create your own power mask—an outside reflection of all the things that make you feel confident inside so that you can fake it until you're confident enough to show the world just how amazing you are. Let's get to it!

What You'll Need

- a store-bought mask (any hard mask will do, you're going to cover it up anyway)

- magazines, printed pictures, and flyers

- paint in different colors

- paintbrush

- glue

- scissors

○ a jar with water (to wash off the paintbrush)

○ old cloth to wipe off your paintbrush

○ any other stuff you'd like to put on your mask—feathers, old pieces of cloth, foil, candy wrappers, and so on

Directions

○ Begin this exercise by thinking about all the things about yourself that make you feel great and confident—if you're having trouble with this step, ask people what they think your strengths are.

○ Once you have a list of your strengths and unique traits, flip through the magazines/pictures/flyers.

○ Cut out any picture, word, shape, or color that you think represents your list of strengths and your uniqueness.

○ Set these pictures aside and get rid of the scrap paper and magazines on your desk.

○ Next, think about a color (or colors) that represent you.

○ Pick up your paintbrush and begin painting your mask in this color (or colors).

○ Allow your mask to dry.

○ Next, begin to layer your pictures, words, shapes, and other cut-out colors onto your mask—you can layer until it feels right to stop or until you believe your mask best represents you.

○ Allow the glue to dry.

○ Finally, add your other stuff—feathers, cloth, foil, and so on.

○ Allow it to dry one last time.

○ Once your mask is completely dry, put it on and look at yourself in the mirror.

○ How does it feel to wear your mask? What does this masked person do that makes them special? Is this masked person confident? Do they love themselves?

This exercise will take a couple of days to finish. Take your time with it as long as you have one week to spend purely on gazing in the mirror and answering the questions above. And remember, this task isn't about being perfect—it's about creating a mask that shows you all of your uniqueness and your strengths.

Week 5 to 9 Timetable

Monday	Tuesday	Wednesday	Thursday	Friday	Saturday	Sunday
Inner Mythbuster		Inner Mythbuster		Inner Mythbuster		
Spoiler Alert It's You	Spoiler Alert It's You	Spoiler Alert It's You	Spoiler Alert It's You	Spoiler Alert It's You	Spoiler Alert It's You	Spoiler Alert It's You
Ultimate Love Triangle	Ultimate Love Triangle	Ultimate Love Triangle	Ultimate Love Triangle	Ultimate Love Triangle	Ultimate Love Triangle	Ultimate Love Triangle

With these exercises, you can begin to build on your self-confidence, learn to love yourself, and start to become comfortable with your growing self-identity. Once you can become confident in yourself, it becomes easier for you to make great choices in the moment, regulate your emotions, and choose which things in your life are important and which just don't deserve your attention.

CHAPTER 4

Under Pressure!

Modern teens like you are under pressure. Some of this pressure is caused by the same stuff your parents and your grandparents went through, such as getting good grades at school, fitting in, and keeping up with chores. But you have other pressures to deal with that the adults in your life didn't have to deal with too, like being unsure about the future because of all the stuff that you're exposed to on the media, social media, FOMO, and so on.

Look, some teens deal with this stuff pretty well, and that's usually because they've learned emotional regulation and self-discipline (I know you're tired of hearing those words)! Other teens aren't doing great with the pressure of modern life, and there's nothing wrong with that. Heck! I'm an adult and even I have trouble coping sometimes!

Let's look at some of the stuff that might be weighing you down. Now, I am going to give you some possible answers or solutions to these things, but we're also going to work on them during your exercises in this section. I'm a firm believer that it's important that you understand why these things are happening, how you can fix them, and learn the skills you need to cope with life right now.

Let's Talk Mental Illness

There's a lot of arguing between adults about the big "M" (mental illness)! Some adults don't think that mental illness exists or that kids have these kinds of problems. Other adults think that it's a very real problem.

Chances are that you grew up with some sort of label attached to you or know of someone who does have a label, such as ADHD, OCD, or ODD—the list goes on and on. Sometimes it feels like kids can't just be kids without there being something wrong with them or giving them a label so that they can take some pills to get better.

Before I carry on, I'm not saying these things don't exist. On the contrary! I think they're scary, real problems teens have to deal with. Where my peeve comes in is that so much attention is on the label and not enough attention is on helping you and giving you the skills to tap into your superpower.

Hold up! Did I say superpower?

Well, yes I did!

Here's a couple of examples. When taught what their superpowers are, teens with ADHD are creative, goal-driven, and critical thinkers. OCD? They're ssk and success-resilient, credtive, and pay ariven, attention teativitThey're h. OD-D? Hyedperfocus,ventuition (spidey senses), passionate, and goal-driven.

You see? Every label comes with great things, but so much focus is placed on the stuff that teens "can't" do because they have a label, disorder, or mental illness. I simply don't believe in the word "can't"—maybe I have ODD too!

So what skills do you need to tap into your personal superpower?

You become a great communicator who can let people know what your needs are. You build good friendships where you support each other, and you learn how to validate your emotions without judgment—don't worry, I'll fill you in on what it means to validate your emotions.

No Pressure—We Wish!

One of the worst pressures you will feel as a teen is peer pressure. Despite what people say, everyone feels like they want to belong to something, and this can sometimes mean we do stuff we're not supposed to do just so that we fit in. Some of these things include drugs, alcohol, and risky behaviors—but again, these are the big bads that adults seem to focus on.

The reality is that when it comes to your friends and the people you go to school with, it's the small, everyday pressures like dressing in a certain way or even taking electives that don't really suit you that can build up until it all feels like it's too much. In the movie *Encanto*, the character Luisa sings a song that describes these small pressures perfectly. Sometimes it's all these small things ("the drip, drip, drip that'll never stop") that make you want to blow up.

And then, of course, there's the pressure to get good grades so that you pass, you're not judged, and your parents stay off your back. You also might have siblings, sports and social commitments, and, and, and, and... Is it any wonder that you feel like it's all too much?

So how do you learn the skills to deal with all of this pressure?

Assertive communication and asking the right questions! I know this step is easier said than done, but I will show you how to do it and still be respectful. Once you know why you're doing what you're doing and can communicate what you need to cope, it becomes much easier to create your own boundaries.

A Word On Tech

Okay, so I'm going to get into tech more in a later chapter, but for now, I'd like to chat about the pressure it can put on you. Before you roll your eyes, I'd like you to really think about what makes you feel great online and what doesn't.

I'm not talking about spending hours scrolling through social media or gaming, because as you will learn later, these activities are basically just ways to avoid doing the stuff you know is good for you but you feel like is too hard—I'm talking about really feeling great about yourself.

A lot of teens, when the adults in their lives aren't around, admit that social media actually makes them feel rotten about themselves, puts pressure on them to be something they're not, or at the very best, has them feeling like they're failing.

Like it or not, social media has a powerful influence over your life—that's why social media famous people are called "influencers"! It makes you believe that you need praise (validation) from the outside world and that unless you have a life like those people on the screen, you're just not good enough.

FOMO and cyberbullying can cause you to feel like something is missing in your life, and a lot of the time, those filters that are designed to keep you safe from the bad stuff just don't work as well as they should. All of this adds pressure to your life, and that isn't a great thing when you're already dealing with everything else!

I don't believe that tech and social media are all bad though. I just don't think teens have been taught how to deal with this pressure or how to build enough confidence for self-validation and pride—but more on that later.

For now, let's get into how you can deal with all of these different pressures and remove the labels of mental illness so that you can become a pro at dealing with stress and saying "no" to pressure!

Rate My Pressure

Before you carry on with your weekly exercises, you need to know what it is that is stressing you out in the first place.

Take a look at the questions below, filling each one in as honestly as you can—try not to think about what is cool or socially acceptable. Rather, take a moment to ask yourself, "Is this something that affects me, or is this something that other people *think* should affect me?"

The Daily Stuff

List five things that put pressure on you or stress you out during the day.

1.

2.

3.

4.

5.

The Major Stuff

List five things, positive or negative, that are major in your life and that are putting pressure or stress on your life. This list could include exams, college, divorce, death, breakups, and so on.

1.

2.

3.

4.

5.

The Life Stuff

List five things that stress you out about your life right now. This list could include something permanent and lasting (like moving, a disability, or a chronic illness) or something more temporary (like fighting in your home or conflicts around religion or culture).

1.

2.

3.

4.

5.

The Good Daily Stuff

List five things that make you feel happy or content every single day.

1.

2.

3.

4.

5.

The Coping Stuff

List five things you do to help you cope when you feel stressed.

1.

2.

3.

4.

5.

Now you know what is causing you stress and pressure in the different areas of your life, what makes you feel good, and how you normally cope when you're not feeling great. These lists are going to help you with the exercises for weeks 10 to 14, so let's dive in.

DBT Exercises Weeks 10 to 14

Exercise 7—I Said What I Said (Dear Man!)

"Dear Man" is an acronym you can use to communicate your needs to other people in a way that is respectful to who you're speaking to and to yourself. For teens like you, sometimes it can be difficult to let people know how you feel without letting your emotions get the better of you.

Here's the thing, when your needs aren't being met, you're more likely to have an emotional response. For teens, that means reacting (unless you've practiced your Taking a Beat exercise).

Let's say you have been practicing Taking a Beat but you're still unsure of how you can say what you need to say... Dear Man!

I'll break it down for you.

D stands for "describe": Here you will try to be clear about the facts of the situation. This means not judging and not using feelings to say what needs to be said. For example, "You're asking for the dishwasher to be emptied in the morning."

E stands for "express": This method of communication is when you can let the other person know how you are feeling about the situation. For example, "With everything else I need to get done before I leave for school, this makes me feel overwhelmed and rushed."

A stands for "assert": Here you create a boundary: "I need to shift my dishwashing chore to later in the day."

R stands for "reinforce": Wait for the other person's response and then act (not react) appropriately. In other words, if they agree, say, "Thank you for hearing me out." If they don't respond, move on to the next letter.

M stands for "mindful": Listen to what the other person is saying without getting into an argument. Remember, they also have needs. Respond only once you understand their needs. For example, "I hear you need me to empty the dishwasher in the morning. Is there another chore I can leave until later so that the dishwasher can get done?"

A stands for "appearance": It's important that you're confident in expressing your needs. This step can be done by staying away from words like "may," "could," "should," and so on. For example, "I hear you need me to empty the dishwasher in the morning. Maybe there is another chore I can leave until later so that the dishwasher can get done?" doesn't sound as confident as "Is there another chore..." Don't worry we're going to work on your confidence some more during later chapters!

N stands for "negotiate": Sometimes the other person is not going to be prepared to budge, and this is where most blow-ups happen because you've been polite, they've been polite, and somehow no one wants to compromise. Negotiating will help both of you come to a better understanding so that everyone wins. For example, "What do you suggest to help me feel less overwhelmed with the morning chores?" This question shifts the responsibility from you to the other person and asks them to empathize with how you're feeling. And you never know—they may come up with a really great idea where both of you lighten the load.

Let's put this exercise into practice now.

Describe

Describe the facts here

Express

Express how you are feeling here

Assert

Assert what you need here

Reinforce

Thank the other person here (or move to the next step)

Mindful

Write what you think the other person's needs are here

Appearance

Write your confidence phrase here

Negotiate

Write your negotiation points here

Exercise 8—"No" Is a Complete Sentence: Dealing With Peer and Adult Pressure

Teens find it tough to say "no" a lot of the time, and there's a good reason for that. Because you're working a whole lot in your feels right now and you want to know that you belong, you may be afraid that you will lose a friend, hurt someone important to you, or be kicked out of a group to wander around as the loner.

These extra layers of big feelings like guilt, fear, and shame can sometimes be the things that have you saying "yes" when really you mean "no."

Here's the thing about saying "no": Even adults suck at it sometimes, and it's so much harder for you to say this simple little word without trying to explain away all the reasons you don't want to do something.

The reality is that "no" is a complete sentence. This fact means you don't really need to explain why something goes against your morals and values or just doesn't sit right with you. But—and this is a *big* BUT—it takes a whole lot of practice to get to the point of saying "no" and not feeling like you need to add all of the whys.

So how do you practice saying "no" or even know when to say "no"? You practice the worksheet below.

What You'll Need

○ this worksheet

○ a chair or a comfortable space to sit and face the pretend person in the room

○ a friend or family member who you trust to practice in the last week of this exercise

○ a timer

Directions

○ Fill in the worksheet below—make sure you are filling in a new worksheet with a different situation every time you complete the exercise.

○ Set your timer for 15 minutes.

○ Take a seat and face an imaginary person in the room.

○ Close your eyes and pretend that the person on your worksheet is present and you're saying no to them.

○ When you are ready, open your eyes and read the situation out loud.

○ Next, read the reasons why you are saying no out loud.

○ Close your eyes again and take a deep breath.

○ Say "no." Practice saying it clearly and with confidence. You don't need to be rude, just assertive.

Worksheet

Tick off the sentences that apply to this situation. Read the ticked-off sentences during your exercise.

Sentence/Reason	Tick for Yes
I can't give you what you are asking for.	
This doesn't feel right for me.	
I will feel terrible about myself if I don't say "no."	
This is wrong/illegal and I will get into trouble if I don't say "no."	
If I say "no," I will get into trouble (homework, chores, responsibilities).	
If I don't say "no," I will regret this.	
It feels right to say "no."	
I understand saying "no" is the right thing to do.	
I don't need to explain why I am saying "no."	

Exercise 9—Time Really Is On Your Side (If Ya Know How)

So you now know how to say "no." The ability to say "no" is super important when dealing with peer pressure as well as the weight of what the adults in your life can sometimes expect from you. You also know how to express your needs and negotiate a win-win for you and the other person.

The next big pressure that affects teens is time! Your schedules are full and it can sometimes feel like you have absolutely no time for yourself. From homework to sports, social commitments, family time, friends, studies, and so on, teens have an enormous amount of stuff to get done. While it's true that teens have the same amount of time as adults in a day, the reality is that kids, in general, have to get more done.

With so much stuff to do, it's only reasonable that you would feel pressured and overwhelmed. One of the biggest issues with all of this is... no one is teaching you how to manage your time.

A while back, I remember watching one of those online videos where a professor was giving a lecture. She stood in front of her class and held up an empty glass jar. She tells the class the empty jar represents a student's time in a day. Next, she holds up a jar of rocks and says, "These are the priority tasks you need to get done." She pours the rocks into the glass jar and asks the class if the jar is full. Most of the class agrees that it is full. Next, the professor holds up a far of pebbles. "These are the daily things you need to get done," she says, and she pours the pebbles into the jar. The pebbles come to rest between the rocks, and, once again, the professor asks if the jar is full. Even more of the class agree that the jar is full. Finally, the professor picks up a jar of sand. "This is your free time. It's your family, friends, gaming, and so on," she says. She pours the sand into the jar and it settles between the remaining gaps. "Now," she exclaims, "the jar is full. But what if I were to pour the sand first, the pebbles second, and the rocks last?" A couple of students step forward and try to pour the contents in a different order, but try as they might, they just can't fit everything in. "You see," said the professor, "if you know how to fill your time properly, a lot can get done!"

This experiment is great because it physically shows you how to manage your time, which is your next task! It's time to build your own time jar.

What You'll Need

- ○ rocks of different sizes

- ○ pebbles or gravel of different sizes

- ○ sand

- ○ four plastic or glass jars, big enough for your experiment

- ○ labels or paper and glue to create your own label

- ○ markers to label your jars

Directions

- ○ Begin your exercise by cleaning your workspace so that it is clutter-free.

- ○ Set out each of your exercise objects.

- ○ Grab your first label and mark it "priority tasks."

- ○ Begin to list your priority tasks on this label. Don't worry if you need an extra label—remember that these should be your priorities and not someone else's. Examples of priority tasks would be chores, hygiene, mental health, homework and studies, time with family, and so on.

- ○ Stick this label on one of the jars.

- ○ Place one rock in the jar for each priority task.

- ○ Grab your next jar and label it "everyday tasks."

- ○ Begin to list your everyday tasks like making your bed, eating healthy, feeding your pets, and so on.

- ○ Place two pebbles in the jar for each everyday task.

- ○ Stick this label to one of the jars.

- ○ Finally, grab another label and mark it "free time."

- ○ Begin to list all of the things you love to do in your free time. This list could include gaming, hanging out with friends, surfing the web, sports clubs, and so on.

- ○ Pour sand into this jar until it is full.

- ○ Now comes the fun part! Fill your empty jar with your rocks first.

- ○ Next, place your pebbles in the jar.

- ○ Finally, pour your sand into the jar.

- ○ Feel free to shake it around a little to get everything to settle.

○ You can even experiment and see if you can fill your jars differently—this can be done every second day by shifting stones and pebbles in and out of your jars to see what the consequences are of you not doing your tasks. Let an adult know that you will be experimenting for three weeks so that they can help you stay on track!

If you have too many priority tasks, you can decide what should go and what can stay—with an adult's advice and help, of course. The same goes for your everyday tasks and your free time.

Now you know what needs to get done first (priority tasks), what should get done every day (everyday tasks), and the rest of it is your free time, teen! Having something visual to guide you can make time management feel so much less overwhelming. And, it allows you to see if you really have too much that *has* to get done or if you're just filling your jar in the wrong order.

Week 10 to 14 Timetable

Monday	Tuesday	Wednesday	Thursday	Friday	Saturday	Sunday
Dear Man!		Dear Man!		Dear Man!		Dear Man!
	Practicing "No"		Practicing "No"		Practicing "No"	
Time Jar		Time Jar		Time Jar		Time Jar
		Revise		Revise		Revise
		Experiment		Experiment		Experiment

Now you have the skills you need to crush the pressure you feel. Having said that, stress and pressure are a really confusing mix of your brain sending you messages and the hormones that put your body into fight or flight mode. Because of this process, it's really important that you speak with an adult if you feel like you're not coping after completing these exercises. You may need a little extra coaching and help with managing your time and learning how to say "no," and that's fine!

CHAPTER 5

Becoming the Boss of You

Teens are stuck in a bit of a puzzling loop. You want to be independent, but you're not sure what it takes to be independent. You want to make decisions for yourself, but being responsible for these decisions is just plain scary. You don't want to be told what to do, but sometimes it's just easier to be told what the next steps are in life.

It's frustrating, overwhelming, and let's face it... as much as we don't like our parents telling us what to do, the thought of having to do it all on our own is terrifying. Teens think that being scared of something means running away, crying, or cowering in a corner. However, in your teen years, fear can look a bit different.

Have you ever spent the entire afternoon gaming when you know you have an important assignment or loads of homework to do? That's fear! Ever totally avoided having to tell someone something important? That's fear. Ever skipped your chores and done literally anything else? That's fear.

All of these examples might sound downright ridiculous, but let me explain.

Adults seem to think teens are lazy when they don't do the stuff that needs to be done, but avoidance is usually a sign of not wanting to take responsibility. Now, what you need to ask yourself is why are you not wanting to do what you're supposed to do.

Sometimes it really is laziness, and in that case, you'll need to learn self-discipline (you have an exercise for it later in this chapter).

Sometimes you forget about the stuff you need to do, and this forgetfulness could be because of two things—disorganization and poor time management or you're subconsciously blocking it out because it's stressing you out and you're avoiding the stress.

But, if you want to be independent or want the adults in your life to be able to trust you to be responsible enough to go at it solo, you're going to have to prove yourself to them. And this is a perfectly reasonable thing to ask of you—to expect that you won't avoid doing the things you're supposed to do, to stop forgetting, and to admit when you need help.

With that in mind, before you can begin to work on your independence exercises, you're going to have to figure out what you're avoiding, what you're afraid of, and what requires self-discipline.

Uncovering Your Responsibility Fears

This worksheet will help you uncover the reasons you're not taking responsibility for the stuff you need to get done. It's super important that you're honest when working through this exercise so that you know what needs self-discipline, what is fear, and what is a time management issue. I've filled in the first line for you so that you can see how to complete the worksheet.

Responsibility/ task	Emotion/action	Opposite action	Reason (fear, self-discipline, time, etc.)
Math homework	I don't do it because I don't understand the work and I'm going to fail anyway.	Ask for help or extra tutoring so that I understand what I'm doing and pass.	Fear of failure.

Now you have a list of the reasons you're not doing the things that need to be done so that you can become independent without fear. But, before we continue with your exercises, let's look at what it means to be independent as a teen.

Teen Independence Unmasked

As a teen, you're going through some pretty neat and sometimes rough changes. These changes include your emotions, body, social, and family relationships, and the things you didn't even think about a couple of years ago suddenly become very real. Understandably, you would find all of these changes overwhelming.

On top of all of these changes, you're very aware of the fact that in just a few short years, you're going to be an adult—and that means you're going to be expected to do just about everything by yourself.

The biggest step toward becoming an adult is learning how to become independent. Being independent means grabbing the metaphorical bull by the horns and proving that you can make good decisions for yourself. It also means exploring your own ideas and opinions, figuring out where you fit into the world, and understanding that the way you think might be different from the way your family and friends think.

Being independent also means that you need to learn how to follow the rules, communicate well with others, and keep your emotions in check. Before you roll your eyes on the rule bit, I want you to know that rules are in place to keep you safe. When you break a rule, chances are that you will feel fearful, guilty, or at the least, worry about the consequences.

If you remember in earlier chapters, we spoke about the fact that the decision-making area of your brain (the PFC) takes a bit longer to catch up when you're a teen. A part of these decision-making skills is called executive functioning.

Executive function is really important and kind of like a prism. It looks like one thing when you hold it up but when you move it around it looks different, and when the light catches it, it's a burst of amazing color that turns an ordinary space into a rainbow. These executive functioning skills are your ability to concentrate, ability to set goals (and work toward them), self-control, problem-solving, and how well you can remember the short-term stuff.

For teens, things problem-solving and concentration aren't an issue unless you have ADHD, but even then, you do have the ability to hyperfocus. Teens can sometimes have an issue with working toward goals and self-control.

There are, of course, easy fixes to these obstacles, and the exercises below will help you with developing your executive functioning skills. This will put you on the right path to confidently working toward your independence.

While you're busy doing these exercises for weeks 12 to 15, I encourage you to sit down with an adult in your life and start to discuss your independence and the challenges adults face with their independence. This conversation will give you a secret weapon (knowledge) about the troubles adults face. And, when you have knowledge early on, you can brainstorm solutions for yourself and test the waters of adulthood in a healthy, safe way.

DBT Exercises Weeks 15 to 19

Exercise 10—Decision Dash: The Art of Making Good Decisions

Decisions are a balancing act. A lot of the time people find themselves stuck when it comes to the choices they need to make because they either don't know how to choose or they're scared the choice they make will be wrong... Yup, there's that fear again!

This problem isn't one that only teens face because adults become stuck in life too, but teens have the added pressure of expectations and thinking that the choices they make for their future are forever. Spoiler alert—they're not!

The beauty of life is that you can change at any moment, totally reinventing yourself and doing something different and new. The art of good decision-making is understanding that everything in life is a balancing act and when you know how to balance stuff, you'll become a master at decision-making.

Take a look at the worksheet below. You can choose to do this exercise interactively with a scale if you like or by simply filling in a separate worksheet for each decision you need to make. Remember to keep your worksheets so that you can look back on the decision you made and see how easy becoming unstuck is when you know how.

What You'll Need

- ○ a balance scale and weights (if you choose an interactive approach)

- ○ a couple of copies of this worksheet

- ○ a journal or file where you can store your worksheets

- ○ a pen

Directions

- ○ Clear your workspace so that it's free of clutter and so that you won't be distracted.

○ Switch off or silence your electronic devices.

○ Grab a copy of your worksheet—make sure that you are only working on one worksheet at a time (one decision not everything all at once).

○ Complete the first section of the worksheet first, moving on to the written part only once you have filled in all five points in each block.

○ I've filled in the first block so that you have an example of what to do.

The decision I need to make is...

Example: I feel my friends are holding me back and that we're doing the same stuff over and over again.

Changing	Not changing	Benefits	Cost
Finding a way to expand my friend circle	The same influence and feeling stuck	Exposed to different cultures and beliefs	I may drift apart from my current friends

Once you have filled in all of the blocks above, you can fill in the statements and questions below. Always remember that the decisions you're making are for *you*. While no one wants to hurt other people, it's important that you understand that you're never going to be happy in life if you're working toward someone else's goals or holding yourself back because someone else is happy being stuck.

The most important reason I want to change is:

If someone told you that you'd be happy and successful if you made this change, would you do it?

What would you do right now to begin your journey to happiness and success?

Exercise 11—Chaos to Control With Self-Discipline

Building self-discipline is like building a house. You need a strong foundation for the structure to be strong. You need four walls that are reinforced and a solid roof to keep you safe from the elements. While you theoretically could move into a house that wasn't properly built yet, it wouldn't be comfortable. A badly built house would be risky because the walls or roof may cave in on you.

But how does this translate to self-discipline? The foundation of your house is your behavior and your willingness to stick to doing the things that you know are required of you. But, having a foundation is not having a house, right? No matter how willing you are, your self-discipline house is not complete without its other elements.

The walls of your house are the small steps you take every day to make sure your self-discipline house is built. These steps could include setting reminders on your phone for your chores or your homework. These small steps are like individual bricks or the framework and lumber used to build the outer structure of your house.

Again, your self-discipline home is not finished and it may look kinda like a home, you're still going to get rained on, cold, and be pretty miserable. Your home is only a home once it has a roof, windows, and doors.

These final parts of your self-discipline home are crucial for you to be happy, comfortable, and safe, and it's the action you take. What do I mean? Well, you know what your behaviors should be, you've set your reminders so that you can take small steps every day, and now you need to *take action*. This step means getting up and doing what needs to be done.

So you've built your house, the roof is on, but you've taken shortcuts by not doing things properly. Your house looks livable from the outside, and may even be comfortable inside while the weather is great and things are going well. At the first sign of bad weather (stress or pressure), the windows are going to cave in, the roof will fly off, and you're going to be as uncomfortable and miserable as you would've been without your house.

For this exercise, you're going to build your self-discipline house and experiment with taking shortcuts and missed actions in real life.

What You'll Need

- ○ two old cardboard boxes

- ○ markers or pens

- ○ paints or other materials to create a mock house

- ○ tape

- ○ scissors

Directions

- ○ Clear your workspace and make sure it's clutter-free.

- ○ Flip your box upside down so that the open side is at the top and the closed side is at the bottom—this is your foundation.

- ○ Cut this box down the seams so that you have four pieces.

- ○ Cut out spaces for your windows and doors—you can become really creative here. Create a front door, a back door, and multiple windows.

- ○ Grab your second box and cut it down the seams—you should have four parts—these will be used to create the pitch and sides of your roof.

- ○ Next, grab your markers.

- ○ On the foundation of your house (the bottom of your main box), list the behaviors you need to become responsible and independent. For example, "My behavior should be to get up when my morning alarm goes off and start my day properly so that I can get to school without rushing."

- ○ Move on to the walls of your house and list the small steps you need to take to create these behaviors. Using the example above, your walls would look like this: "*Get out of bed, have my morning drink, make my bed, do five minutes of meditation, brush my teeth, wash my face, get dressed, check my school bag, do my chores, leave the house by 8:15 am.*"

- ○ You can place multiple steps on one wall but try to group them together. For example, "getting out of bed" and "making my bed" could be on one wall, "brushing my teeth," "washing my face," and "getting dressed" on another, "doing my chores" and "checking my school bag" on another, and so on.

- ○ Set these pieces aside and grab your roof, door, and window pieces.

- ○ Label these pieces "Action Taken"—these will be the movable pieces you add as you develop the good actions you need to become independent.

○ Now you can get creative, painting your house however you want, adding decorative pieces to it, and making each piece unique.

○ During your time slots, you can begin to construct your house.

○ Loosely tape the sides of your house to your foundation—three pieces of tape per house side should be fine (one for each side and one for the middle).

○ Next, construct your roof, taping the sides of it together so that it is a complete unit that has a pitch and two sides.

○ Lift the sides of your house and place your roof on it—this should keep your house sturdy and upright.

○ Stick your windows and doors to the structure.

○ Now, when you're sitting down to do your house activity daily, take a moment to look at your house.

○ Have you completed everything that needs to be done to keep your ceiling on and your walls stable?

○ If not, remove one extra, like a door and window for every action you have not taken.

○ If you have not completed any actions, remove your roof.

○ Now, answer these questions:

1. Do you see how your structure falls down?

2. Do you see how the walls fall outward and the windows and door are no longer present?

3. How have the shortcuts and non-actions you've taken today affected your life?

4. Do you have extra things you now need to get done tomorrow?

5. How does this add to your stress and pressure?

6. If you were an outsider looking in, would you think that your actions reflect responsibility and independence?

7. What can you do right now, and tomorrow, to make sure the walls, ceilings, and roof of your house remain firm?

Exercise 12—Teen Daredevil: Healthy Risks for Growth

It's normal for teens to want to take risks. Risks are where you find your identity, let you know what your limits are, and uncover your strengths and weaknesses. Some adults might view risk-taking as being rebellious but there is a difference between good risks and bad risks.

Let's start with the bad risks. Drinking, taking drugs, vaping, smoking, unprotected sex, and being in places you know are unsafe are all examples of bad risks. Deciding to do these things comes with a conscious decision to break the rules, and you're probably going to justify all the reasons you're doing these things. "I'll only try it once. All my friends are doing it," or "What's the worst that can happen?" are ways you could explain away the bad risks you take. The thing about taking bad risks is that they make you feel terrible—perhaps not at the moment, but afterward, when the guilt, shame, or fear of getting caught sinks in, you just don't feel great.

Good risks, on the other hand, make you feel great! They may still have you feeling nervous or excited in the moment, but instead of being filled with guilt or shame afterward, your self-pride, confidence, and sense of independence increase.

Here's an example of a good risk. When you were younger, you needed to learn to ride a bicycle. It took courage to know that your training wheels weren't there to keep you upright, and your parents probably knew that at some point during your first ride, you were going to fall over, skin your knee, or have to deal with not staying upright. But, you and your parents took the risk anyway. You probably fell, screamed, and were terrified, but eventually, your parents let go and you learned to ride your bike. The reward of you increasing your cognitive and gross motor skills, and increasing your confidence was far greater than the risk of you riding with safety wheels your whole life.

Healthy risks are the things that help you to grow in life and give you the skills you need to become a confident, independent adult. The great news about healthy risks as a teen is that most of the healthy risks you will take won't end up with a skinned knee. But, every risk comes with a downside—even the healthy ones—and you're going to have to learn to live with these outcomes.

For most healthy risks, the downside is that you could fail or be disappointed. Now, if you've read any of my other books you will know that failure is not fatal. It's a learning tool that can be used for you to get better in life. People build failure up until it becomes this invisible zombie apocalypse that is going to sweep over them, turning them into a loser.

The worksheet below will help you to decide on what healthy risks you could take in your life and show you how these healthy risks can help you develop and grow.

What You'll Need

- ○ a copy of your worksheet

- ○ a pen or pencil

- ○ your journal or file so that you can reflect on the exercise at the end of every week

Directions

- ○ Answer the questions below as honestly as you can.

- ○ Once a week, review your answers and the actions you've taken.

- ○ Track your progress over the next three weeks.

- ○ At the end of the three weeks, fill in the worksheet labeled "Results."

Healthy Risk Analysis

Question	Answer
What makes you the happiest?	
What's the most valuable thing in the world to you?	
When you think about it, what really excites you?	
If you had all the time in the world, what would you do?	
If you weren't scared, what's one thing would you do?	
What physical thing (sport, skill, instrument, and so on) have you always wanted to try?	
List something new you would like to try.	
How much time will you dedicate to this activity?	
When will you start this new activity/ skill/change?	
What equipment and tools do you need to start this new thing?	
Do you need help or assistance to try this new thing?	
How long will you commit to this new activity?	

Weekly Review Worksheet

This worksheet should be completed once a week so that you can see how you're doing with your good risk. As always, be honest with yourself. If you're avoiding the exercise, why not try and build a self-discipline house to encourage action?

Question	Answer
What steps did you take this week to incorporate your new skill/activity/life change?	
Did you fail, make mistakes, or become frustrated while trying this new thing for yourself?	
What do you think you have learned from failing, making mistakes, or becoming frustrated?	
Were you resilient, pushing yourself through the challenges and obstacles you faced during this week?	
What will you do differently in the week to come so that you can improve and become more confident with this new thing you're trying?	

Taking healthy risks, committing to action, and making good decisions for yourself are all really important steps in becoming independent. Becoming a grown-up and having to be completely responsible for yourself doesn't need to be scary if you know how to navigate these three important aspects of adulthood.

Weeks 15 to 19 Timetable

Monday	Tuesday	Wednesday	Thursday	Friday	Saturday	Sunday
Chaos to Control		Chaos to Control		Chaos to Control		
Teen	Teen	Teen	Teen	Teen	Teen	Daredevil
Daredevil	Daredevil	Daredevil	Daredevil	Daredevil	Daredevil	Review
Decision	Decision	Decision	Decision	Decision	Decision	Dec-Dash
Dash	Dash	Dash	Dash	Dash	Dash	Review

Before you move on to the next chapter, there's one more super important thing you need to know, and that's listening to what others have to say. I'm not talking about pressure, I'm speaking about taking a moment to try and understand what someone is telling you without getting defensive or wanting to argue.

All of the previous exercises and worksheets you've completed are designed to help you filter out what is important, keep your emotions in check, and help you to communicate your needs properly. But, none of this work will help if you're not going to listen to the advice that you're given. Pick trusted adults and mentors that you can speak with that can give you helpful advice and try this advice out.

You never know... You may end up learning something that unlocks your superpowers much quicker!

CHAPTER 6

Screentime and Dreamtime— Navigating a Digital World

The digital world can be amazing—I'm not going to deny that. However, as someone who has spent a fair amount of time online, I also know that it's a complicated space to be in.

My personal opinion is that modern teens are more equipped to handle pressure and FOMO than previous generations. Having said that, it doesn't lessen the confusion about balancing out how much screen time or what should be done online and what shouldn't.

A couple of teens I spoke with said they spend a few hours online every day moving between TikTok, Snapchat, Instagram, and texting apps. Most of them see this behavior as normal for teens but a lot worry about the downsides of using tech. What's different about this new generation of teens is that they know how to keep themselves safe from content they don't want to see (for the most part anyway). But, there's still online bullying and information overload to cope with.

What modern teens and I do agree on is that technology brings people closer—your friend moved away? Facetime and text make it feel like they're still very much present... Or does it?

After chatting to teens, I've come to realize that it's the balance that most teens are battling with. On some deeper level, teens feel like they have lost the essence of a real relationship, and they're not wrong. So how do you fix this?

Digital Decisions—Knowing Where to Start

Social media and texting apps can definitely be used to reduce loneliness and stay in touch with people. However, it can also become an escape from speaking with people face to face.

Have you ever played a game of hide and seek and hid in plain sight, only to be the last person to be found? Being online is kind of the same concept. You can become so used to the comfort of never having to speak with people in real life that you convince yourself online interaction is better.

A lot of the time, this digital game of hide and seek comes from a fear of being rejected or made fun of. In the real world, you need to actually see people and experience all of the unpleasant emotions that come with someone not wanting to be around you. Online? Well, it's still unpleasant but the blow is less harsh and you have more power in taking action—block and delete, right?

The problem with all of this online behavior is that you actually need human interaction on a physical level. Physical touch, reading facial expressions and body language, and watching for other cues are part of your human evolution skills. They let you know if you're safe, wanted, or belong. These things can't be seen or experienced through a screen or in a text.

But like I said, I don't believe in no screen time or severely limited screen time (unless that's what you want, of course). You need to know what your limits are when it comes to spending time online as well as what makes you feel good, what is messing with your head to *make* you feel good, and what is making you feel terrible.

Uncovering Online Behaviors

Fill in the worksheet below. Be super honest about these answers.

Question	Answer
How much time do you spend online every day?	
What apps are you on the most? List these apps from the most time spent to the least time spent, and don't forget video games and content creation for apps like TikTok.	
When you're with your friends in real life, how much time do you spend speaking with them and how much time do you spend on your phone? A percentage is fine for this question.	
What apps make you feel great about yourself, which ones do you use out of habit, which ones do you use to avoid life, and which ones make you feel rotten? Be honest with this section (especially the part about avoiding life).	
How do you feel when you're not allowed to use tech or your favorite apps? Do you get angry, feel panicked, isolated, or is it just a case of, "Meh, I'll just hang out with my friends."	

If the internet went down for seven whole days, what would you do with your time? How do you think you would feel? Do you think your life would change?

What are the advantages of being online? How does online life make things easier? What would you really miss about being online?

What are the disadvantages of being online? What are the parts about being online that you don't like or that you wouldn't miss?

How much time do you think you should be spending online every day? (Your answer should exclude school and research.)

Once you have the answers to these questions, you can do the exercises below. And don't worry—I'm not going to force you to go offline. I'm simply going to give you the tools you need to cope with being online and how to balance your digital life.

Becoming Internet Awesome—Smart Online Choices for Teens

News travels fast when you're online, and it's important that you know how to become internet awesome, make smart choices online, and know when to give that amazing brain of yours a well-deserved break.

The first thing you need to do is draw on your newly learned communication skills so that you can chat *openly* about what is happening online. Speak with your parents and treat online communication in the same way you would face-to-face communication. If you wouldn't say something to a person while they were standing in front of you, please don't say it when you're online.

Remember that not everyone online is who they say they are. There are a lot of fakes out there who are looking for people to con or cause harm. The only way around these people is to communicate about who you're talking to. Most adults have already developed their spidey senses and can spot these fakes quicker than you can say, "cheap knockoff!"

While we're on the topic of communication and scam artists, as you get older, you'll have more access to banking and online commerce products. This access is great because it means you're becoming more independent, but it also means keeping your information and your parents' information safe on the internet. Change your passwords often, make sure they have symbols and numbers in them, and don't use obvious stuff like your birthday for important sites.

Always remember that when you're in doubt about something online, or you're just not coping, talk about it in real life with someone who can guide you through the maze that is online life.

Use the skills you're going to be taught in this chapter while keeping in mind that the Internet is huge! Larger, in fact, than anything else you will ever need to navigate in your life, and it's fine to ask for help and guidance when you need it.

DBT Exercises Weeks 20 to 24

Exercise 13: From Influenced to Influencer—Setting Online Boundaries With Kindness

Setting online boundaries is not too different from setting boundaries in real life. These invisible borders keep you safe and make sure that your mental and physical health are not put in any danger.

What is different between online and real life is that sometimes you can forget there is a person holding the screen or controller. And, when you forget this very important fact, you can become mean or say things you'd never say in real life. You'll need to remember that even if it's just you interacting with the internet, you're still a person—and you can be mean to yourself.

Comparing yourself to others, allowing that nasty voice in your head to tell you that you're not good enough, or wishing away your life to have someone else's are just some examples of not treating yourself with kindness. The internet might be a place of fantasy and fiction a lot of the time but the one undeniable fact is that there is *always* a human involved and people deserve to be treated with kindness—you included!

With that information out of the way, there's another thing I'd like to talk about that deserves some kindness when it comes to online use. I'd like you to take a minute to close your eyes and imagine a supercomputer.

This computer is housed on the top floor of a building and is the smartest and quickest piece of machinery ever invented. It has a storage capacity of 1 petabyte (that's over 1,000 terabytes) and has over a trillion connections coming in and going out of it. It processes information at an astounding speed of 11 million bits per second and provides this info to users at 50 bits per second. And, this incredible computer only needs 10 watts to power it (your computer needs around 100 watts). There's no other computer like this one to have ever been invented and modern technology is hundreds of years away from being able to make anything like this computer. Somehow, you're the owner of this valuable piece of machinery and that means you need to take care of it but also that you can use it whenever you want to.

Wouldn't that be amazing?

What if I told you this supercomputer exists, and it's your brain?

That's right! All of the stats that I gave you above are real! The human brain is amazing and it processes a whole lot of information every second of every day. How much information you put into your brain, or what you decide to program your brain with, is entirely up to you. But, your supercomputer needs to rest from time to time, and just like any other computer, it needs to be protected with a decent firewall, antivirus program, and software encryption.

What You'll Need

- ⭕ your worksheet

- ⭕ your affirmation cards

- ⭕ scissors

- ⭕ tape

- ⭕ a pen or pencil

- ⭕ your journal or file to store your worksheet for weekly reflection

Directions

- ⭕ Cut out your affirmation cards, or copy the sayings and store them in a safe space or with your worksheet.

- ⭕ Clear away extra paper and clean up your workspace.

- ⭕ Fill in your worksheet and be honest with your answers.

- ⭕ File away your daily worksheets in your journal or in a file so that you can review any patterns during the week.

- ⭕ At the end of every exercise, say your affirmations out loud.

Question	Answer
How much time did you spend online today?	
What apps did you use while you were online today?	
Was there anything you saw online today that made you feel good about yourself?	

Was there anything you saw online today that made you feel uncomfortable or bad about yourself?

What feelings did you have when you saw these things online? Guilt, shame, jealousy, anger, and so on?

Why is it important for you to be on apps that don't make you feel good about yourself?

What do you think you can do about limiting your time on these apps?

What rules would you put in place for someone else if they told you an app made them feel terrible?

Can you live without this app? If you can, what are the reasons why you're not deleting or blocking the app?

If you can't delete the whole app, what can you do to protect yourself from the content that makes you feel bad? Block the creator or channel, install a safety or age filter, and so on?

If you can delete apps that feel wrong for you, I suggest you do. Take notice of how you're feeling about deleting this app and record it in your journal or reflection page. If you're being bullied online, make sure to report the content and speak with an adult. Alternatively, switch comments off for your content so that you remove the power from the trolls.

Once you have completed your worksheet, grab your affirmations and repeat them out loud.

1. I need boundaries because they make me feel safe.

2. I don't need to watch or read content that makes me feel bad.

3. It's not my responsibility to comment on anything.

4. Boundaries can feel uncomfortable at first but I will feel better being safe.

5. I need to set limits to protect my brain and my thoughts.

6. Healthy boundaries are not selfish.

7. Boundaries allow me to flourish in a digital world.

Exercise 14: FOMO to JOMO and YOLO

FOMO is a real issue for teens. You don't want to feel like you're left in the dark, but you also know that you can't be physically present at everything! That's what tech is for, right?

Wrong!

FOMO is a real problem that is taking the world by storm, and tech has only made it worse because everyone's stuff always seems to be available all of the time. On top of that, people post the best of their lives and it leaves you thinking, *Why can't I have it all, do it all, wake up in the morning looking like a million dollars....?*

Spoiler alert! Influencers also wake up looking like they went to battle with a blackberry bush and lost—their content is curated!

What you're going to learn with this exercise is how to shift those feelings of FOMO to the joy of missing out (JOMO) or you only live once (YOLO). Imagine, for a minute, that you're scrolling through social media and you see some kids from school setting up for a big party at the lake. You know it's not your thing, and that you'd rather be hanging out with your friends at the mall. Usually, you'd feel pressure to go to the lake or feel a little bit of jealousy, but this time you're happy for the people who are going to the party and happy for yourself because you get to do the stuff you really want to do.

Now, let's say a couple of your friends you wanted to go to the mall with are going to the party... Instead of feeling upset, you understand that they are having their own YOLO moment, and you tell them to have fun while you go off to the mall. This type of response is called emotional maturity, and it comes with something amazing— inner peace! And you can shift FOMO to JOMO pretty easily—if you know how.

What You'll Need

- a large piece of cardboard, paper, or a mirror or wall that you can stick Post-Its or sticky notes to

- Post-Its or sticky notes

- a pen or marker

- your journal or file to record your actions or decisions

Directions

- Clear your workspace and make sure it is clutter-free.

- Stick your piece of cardboard or paper to the wall, if you're using them. If not, move to the next step.

- Grab your sticky notes or Post-Its and lay them out on your workspace individually.

- Choose four notes and write one letter on each one—FOMO.

○ Now, do the same for another four notes—JOMO.

○ And finally, another four notes—YOLO.

○ Stick these notes on your paper, board, wall, or mirror, with FOMO on the left, JOMO on the right, and YOLO at the bottom—they should form an upside-down triangle.

○ On individual sticky notes or Post-Its write the following phrases:

- I did the things I wanted to do and that made me happy.

- I went online to check I didn't miss anything.

- I limited my time/switched off social media because it made me feel bad.

- I compared my life to someone else's online.

- I blocked/silenced apps/people that made me feel bad.

- I was mindful of my thoughts.

- I treated myself with kindness.

- I felt stress/anxiety/depression when online.

- I did something others think is nerdy but I love.

- I checked my phone/notifications every few minutes.

- I sat in front of someone but was on my phone.

- I logged on, scrolled for a few seconds, and logged off.

- I decided to be present.

- I paid attention to how I was feeling while online.

- I took selfies/food/location pictures and posted them immediately.

- I wondered if I was addicted to social media.

○ I got lost on social media/YouTube.

○ I decided I need a digital detox.

○ Once you have written all of these phrases out, place them under the headings FOMO, JOMO, and YOLO—there's no right or wrong answer here. Simply place the notes where you think they should go.

○ Spend five minutes every day evaluating your online use by using the notes you've made.

○ Move the notes around on your board so that they represent how your time online is making you behave and feel. For example, "I went online to check I didn't miss anything" (FOMO), "I decided to be present" (JOMO), and "I blocked/silenced apps/people that made me feel bad" (YOLO).

○ Make a note in your journal or file for Sunday review. This note should include what actions you'll take in the coming weeks to move FOMO items over to JOMO and YOLO.

Exercise 15: Unplug to Power Up!

The thought of unplugging and going offline is really scary for some people. If you're afraid of offline time, don't beat yourself up. In one study, 70% of teens said they were scared to unplug and 40% said they thought they were addicted to social media (Choudhary, 2015). That's a lot of young people suffering from a whole lot of FOMO!

I want you to know this isn't your fault. Social media and the internet are designed to pull you in and keep you trapped. All of this happens on a neurological level which means your digital devices are speaking directly to your brain without you knowing about it. I'm not going to go into a whole science lesson here, but what I will tell you is that being online and gaming releases a happy chemical in your brain called dopamine. This chemical is the one that rewards your brain for good behavior, even when you know that what you're doing might not be the best thing for you. So when you go online, even when the stuff you're watching makes you feel bad, dopamine is rewarding your brain. This "reward" is how any addiction forms—it's a trap that you only know about once you're in it. So how do you get out of this trap? You slowly untangle yourself from it!

The way to start untangling yourself is to start giving that amazing supercomputer brain of yours a rest. Some people call this a digital detox but I think this phrase is a bit extreme—unless you are addicted, of course, and then you'll need to get professional help for your addiction.

You see, your brain has so many layers and abilities that all need attention and this means giving attention to all of these things—going outdoors, getting creative, listening to music, spending time with people face-to-face, and so on.

In this exercise, you're going to learn how to unplug in small, manageable chunks as well as learn to live without the apps and channels that aren't great for your mental health.

What You'll Need

- ○ the worksheet, printed

- ○ a pen or pencil

Directions

- ○ Fill in the worksheet below as honestly as you can.

- ○ Stick this worksheet up where it can be seen.

- ○ Take action! Remember, nothing works if you don't take action and change something.

Question	Answer	Alternative
What is the average time you spent on social media/ gaming this week?		Write what you could do.
How much time did you actually want to spend on social/media gaming?		Write the difference here.
What three apps did you spend the most time on this week and why?		What three activities make you forget about being online?
If you're scrolling social media/gaming in your free time, how much free time do you have?		If you were to use this free time to actively do something, what would it be?
What time did you begin going online/gaming and what time did you stop?		If you practiced self-care in this time, what would you do?
What rules did you break when you were online/ gaming this week?		What rules do you want to follow when you're online/ gaming?
If you had a do-over, what would you have done differently this week?		What action will you take this weekend that helps you act differently?

You will complete this exercise only once per week, on a Friday, but you're going to try and unplug by doing whatever it is that you've written in your "Alternatives" column on a Saturday and Sunday. So, if you said you spent three hours per day online just aimlessly scrolling, creating selfies, and so on, and your alternative would've been to study, go for a hike, and have face-to-face contact with your friends... then this is what you're going to do on the weekend. In other words, your alternatives column is the actions you're going to take to help you unplug, give your supercomputer a much-needed update, and recharge your brain.

Weeks 20 to 24 Timetable

Monday	Tuesday	Wednesday	Thursday	Friday	Saturday	Sunday
Influencer	Influencer	Influencer	Influencer	Influencer		
FOMO to JOMO	FOMO to JOMO	FOMO to JOMO	FOMO to JOMO	FOMO to JOMO	FOMO to JOMO	FOMO to JOMO
Unplug to Power Up				Unplug to Power Up	Unplug to Power Up	Unplug to Power Up

And that's it, teen, you have all of the critical skills you need to begin to navigate the world on your terms. Remember, you need to take action once you've decided to do something because, without action, nothing is ever going to change or get done.

I'd like to encourage you to not skip over the conclusion. There's one last super fun, useful surprise in store for you. See you on the flip side.

Conclusion

We've reached the end of this epic DBT journey, teen. Congratulations on taking action, regulating your emotions, communicating your needs, and developing your independence. You're well on your way to becoming a mindful master of your own universe.

But guess what?

The adventure doesn't end! In fact, it's just the beginning of your superhero story where you learn to harness your personal power. With the skills you've been taught, you have earned your cape and can tackle what life throws at you with humor and grace. Remember, life is a quest and you'll learn and grow every single day—if you allow yourself to.

There is so much more to explore, so much amazingness, and incredible beauty beyond your screens. You have the key that unlocks the door to a happier, healthier you, and now it's up to you to put that key in the door, turn the key, and begin the first day of the rest of your life.

Spoiler Alert!

Your reading isn't done just yet. A bonus chapter awaits you where we'll dive into three extra skills that will elevate you from mere superhero to Master Chief! With goal setting, emotional reflection, mindfulness, and tips and tricks to accelerate the effectiveness of your DBT worksheets and activities, your *free* bonus chapter helps you make the most of your DBT toolkit.

Get ready to master your emotional universe, become the captain of your own ship, and the navigator of your unique story! With these extra tools and skills, you won't just navigate the world, you'll conquer every decision you need to make with maturity, confidence, and self-pride.

Always remember, you are not alone in life. There are others who have walked your path, those who want to walk it with you, and trusted adults who can offer you a hand up along the way.

Now, as you turn this final page, I'd love for you to do so with the knowledge that you have the power to face obstacles and challenges with resilience. Mistakes and setbacks are great because they allow you to learn and tap into the wisdom you already have buried inside you.

Stay awesome, stay resilient, and never stop believing in your inner power, teen!

Made in the USA
Las Vegas, NV
06 June 2025

23275063R00057